Introduction

This easy to read guide is meant to help you buy wholesale and closeout kids related merchandise in New York.

I have a wholesale business in New York, www.closeoutexplosion.com, which is located near the New York Fashion District.

Through my business, I have bought and sold hundreds of thousand of dollars worth of wholesale children's merchandise.

The market for kids' products is tremendous, and New York is one of the best places to purchase wholesale and closeout merchandise.

I am happy to share this valuable information with you.

Please make sure to perform your own research, as well as seek professional advice, before making any business decisions.

I am happy to try to help you to the best of my ability.

You are welcome to contact me with any questions or comments, as well as visit my warehouse the next time you are in New York.

Chapter 1

New York's Top Toy Distributors

New Dragon Toy Wholesale Inc, 101 W 27th St Frnt 1, NY 10001, +1212-691-8676. This is among the biggest stores in New York that manufactures and sells toys in wholesale. The store has been operational for the last 25 years specializing in assorted toys ranging from cars to dolls with unbeatable prices and very friendly attendants.

Shepher Distributors, 2300 Linden Blvd, NY 11208, +1718-927-6700. The Shepher Distributors has been operational for 72 years dealing in toys, dolls, games and sports items. The store only deals in wholesale distribution not only in New York and the USA but they also do shipping to everywhere around the world. They have a stock of over 7000 different toys. Ideal Trading USA Inc, 58-30 Grand Ave, Maspeth, NY 11378, USA, +1718-366-8860. This store has been in existence for a while with a variety of children friendly toys and sports items at affordable prices. They are committed to stocking and selling high quality and durable toys. They have an excellent team of salespeople. Toy Connection Inc, 22 Lawrence Ln#1, Lawrence, NY 11559, USA, +1516-371-9206. Toy

Connection has been in business for over 20 years and still counting, they have high-quality assorted toys and novelties at very affordable prices. They stock seasonal toys like easter eggs, party toys and artificial tattoos as well as school items.Great Toys Inc, 3409 Queens Blvd #3, Long Island City, NY 11101, USA, +1718-784-8987.

Great Toys is a manufacturing and wholesaling store that has operated for over a decade. Their quality range of teddy bears and other stuffed animals are relatively affordable.Elco Toys, 378 Cleveland St, Brooklyn, NY11208, USA, +1718-788-2188. The store stocks a variety of high quality toys stuffed animals and teddy bears. Their prices are pocket-friendly. They are committed to supplying the best in the market. They also have excellent, friendly and very helpful staff.Mezco Toyz LLC, 3738 13St, Long Island City, NY 11101, USA, +1718-472-5100. This particular store is known for stocking and selling quite a variety of the best of the living dead dolls inspired from books, comics, movies and TV series, some of them include Marvel, Batman, Spiderman, Thor among others including Halloween themes.

Closeout Services Corporation, 380 Rector Pl #6e, New York, NY 10280, USA. Closeout store stocks assorted toys, dolls and gifts. They pride themselves in selling high-quality products at very pocket-friendly prices. They not only sell in the USA but also ship their products all over the world, they have put in place secure online payments and fast shipping techniques that always leave their clients satisfied.Mastermedia Deals, 1908 Coney Island Ave, Brooklyn, NY 11230, USA. They have been operational for more than three decades buying millions of products at relatively low prices and selling them to retailers at affordable prices making the retailers realize quite high profits.Galaxy Distributors, 1691 Church St # B, Holbrook, NY 11741, USA, +1631-563-3990. The Galaxy distributors deal with a variety of other high-quality items besides toys. Their toys include balls, magic cubes and super fighter jets. Their items are very cheap although one has to make a minimum order of $100 in a single purchase. They also offer free shipping to purchases above $250, their online store runs offers on assorted items from time to time.

Chapter 2

10 Popular Wholesale Boutique Brands Of Children's Clothing

There are many companies that manufacture clothes for kids. Retailers are advised to conduct research before purchasing wholesale brands. One of the things retailers need to understand is that not all these brands will meet buyers' needs. There are endless chain stores that stock cute items. Here are the 10 Popular Boutique Brands of Children's Clothing.

1. Joules

Joules is a Britain based brand. The brand comprises of fun skirts, beautiful dress and soft tees among other outfits. The clothes are characterized by bright colors that have made them more popular among children. The patterns and quality is undeniable.

2. Appaman

The brand designs wonderful outerwear for girls and boys, funky prints as well as graphic tees among others. The clothes from this designer are versatile such that they can be used for formal and casual events.

3. Pink Chicken

The pink chicken children dresses, leggings and tees are irresistible to buyers. The outfits have been designed for both formal and informal occasions. The dresses fall between 50 to $70 price range when purchase on wholesale. The brand also includes skirts and other outfits that will make kids look adorable.

4. Wes and Willy

Retailers targeting customers who love traditional styles need to stock products from Wes and Willy. The company manufactures polos and tees among other outfits for children of different ages. The clothes are characterized by different features including skulls, drum sets and cross bones among others.

5. Zutano

Zutano is one of the most popular brands when it comes to children's clothing. The brand is characterized by cozy and colorful designs. The clothes from this designer are fun as well as unique. Some of the common designs incorporate flowers, dinosaurs, stripes and vehicles among others. Most of the products from this designer are versatile such that they can be used by both boys and girls. Retailers who want to attract buyers that prefer fashionable and trendy need to go for Zutano.

6. Tea

The tea collection comprises of clothes for kids aged between aged between 6 and 12 years. The high quality of clothes from this designer makes them ideal for daily playwear. Some of the common children's clothes from this company include graphic tees, leggings, dresses and cargo pants. The clothes are sold at an affordable price thus making them ideal for low and average income earners.

7. Hilly Chrisp

There is no better gift to present to kids than Hill Chrip dress or leggings. The brand has mixed patterns and colors. Most buyers prefer quality bloomers and shorts. The clothes are sold at an affordable price on wholesale.

8. Kissy Kissy

Kissy Kissy designs clothes in different sizes and colors. The clothes portray different theme including separates, fire trucks as well as flowers. The clothes from this brand can be used on various occasions.

9. Hartstrings

Hart strings are a perfect choice for people who want quality and affordable clothing for special occasions. The firm designs classic khakis, twirling dresses, critter bottoms and tops as well as madras.

10. Petit Bateau

The brand has been offering high quality and affordable dresses for kids. Petit Bateau is known for infant rompers, classic cotton sweaters and undergarments that retailers are not likely to find elsewhere.

Chapter 3

10 New York Baby Wear Wholesalers

You may be wanting to start a babywear retail store or you want to get new suppliers for your shop but you don't know where to start off. This list of top 10 New York baby wear wholesalers will help you locate a baby wear wholesaler in New York, plus their contact address.

NYKidsMarket has over 25 showrooms that stocks over 250 kids and baby brands on their premises. The showrooms are owned by different individuals. Therefore, you will get some stocking clothes only while others stock baby accessories or a combination of both. NYKidsMarket holds semi-annual Market Weeks in which they offer their clients special promotions and discounts. NYKidsMarket is located at 34 West 33rd Street. Their email address is nyckidsmarket@gmail.com.

Babyking is another babywear wholesaler. Their two showrooms are located at 182-20 Liberty Avenue Jamaica, which also is their headquarters, and the Manhattan Showroom located at 1384 Broadway at the corner of 38th street. They only sell to business and the minimum you can order is $1000. Babyking stocks babywear such as blankets, booties, layette, socks, shoes and clothing for winter. Their telephone number is 800 424 2229 or 718 465 6857. However, for you to get into the showrooms, you need to send an email to bkjay@msn.com to set up an appointment.

Weeplay Kids stocks babywear themed on three famous brands, namely, Buster Brown, Marilyn Monroe and Hello Kitty. Weeplay has teams of workers that manufacture their merchandise. They are located at 25 West 39th Street 5th Floor. Their telephone number is 212 563 2022. Their email address is info@weeplaykids.com.

Another place where you can buy babywear on wholesale is Andy & Evan. They stock clothes for children between 0-14 years of age. Their corporate showroom is located at 261 West 35th Street, Suite 702. To place an order or to set up an appointment at their showroom, email them at sales@andyandevan.com.

Kids Wholesale Warehouse Clothing has a warehouse in New York where they sell clothes in small wholesale packs of three to four mixed sizes and colors. Their minimum order value is $100. They stock brands such as American Vintage, Angels, Baby Lulu and Crayon Kids. They are located at 44 Glenridge Lane. To place an order email them at kidswearhouse@gmail.com or call 585 672 1316

Rachel Riley is a British clothing brand with a shop at 401 Broadway, Suite 709, New York. This clothing shop stocks babywear ranging from dungarees, girl dresses, trousers, babygros, knitwears to footwear. Their email address is mailorder@rachelriley.com.

Another babywear wholesaler you can order your merchandise from is BabyVision. Located in the Hudson Valley, this company manufactures three clothing brands namely, Hudson Baby, Luvable Friends and Yoga Sprout. To order from them, email them at orders@babyvision.com.

The East End Shirt Company sells baby onesies at their showroom located at 3 Mill Creek Road, Port Jefferson. Their email address is info@eastendco.com.

Lucky Jade Kids is another wholesaler stocking baby clothes such as rompers, dresses, hats and blankets. They have over ten stores in New York. Email them at customerservice@luckyjadekids.com for more information.

Last but not least is Marmellatta Children's Wear which manufactures and sells baby clothes in wholesale. They are located at 1333 Broadway Street. Their telephone number is 212 594 7400

Chapter 4

10 Children's Clothing Showrooms In NYC

Whether you are looking to stock up your store with additional brands of children's clothing, or are looking to import a new brand of wholesale kids clothes into your market, New York has many showrooms that you can visit.

Below is a list of 10 showrooms in New York that specialize in brand name and boutique label fashions for kids.

1. At **TaROO Too** which is on the Upper East Side, you can see gorgeous clothes and gifts for both boys and girls. They include brands like Mudpie, Lemon and Charlie Rocket and the prices start as low as $8. Cute tutus, hoodies, winter jackets…you choose! Located at 1490 1st Avenue.

2. **Babesta Threads** is the spacey 450 square feet showroom for things that kids absolutely love! It is on 56 Warren St., and it has Eazy Bean chairs, Junk Food concert shirts, Uglydolls and even clothes with a vintage and unique charm. The target is mostly for younger than 6, but the owners have also included the Chaos Recycled brand.

3. In **Sweet William** the fashion entrepreneur Bronagh Staley personally took care of the handpicks, all accessories and clothes for all ages – from newborns up

until the age of 8. Kids will admire the brands like Wovenplay or April Showers. Located at 324 Wythe Ave Brooklyn.

4. If you and your kids love Japanese-style cute clothes and accessories, then check out **Bit'Z Kids,** on 410 Columbus Ave. You will be overwhelmed with the cuteness of endless colors of toys and clothes in Japanese style. The showroom also has a play area, making it convenient for moms shopping with their kids.

5. And for those really interested in the latest hip trends, **Level 2**, located in Park Slope neighborhood, 1491 2nd Ave. you will be stunned to see that the clothes are intended for under 15-year old kids. Gorgeous pattern dresses, knitwear with patterns, cute bags and brands such as Miss Behave, or bright cute shirts of Stella Blu, even some jeans and denim wear from Tractr. Sunglasses, wallets...it is endless!

6. When you enter **Torly Kid**, located on 51 Hudson St., you will understand the idea that owner Carol Adams had. First named Babylicisous and now Torly Kid, this showroom has items for tots and tweens both. You will stumble upon adorable lines like Lunchbox, Tooby Doo or Appaman. The greatest thing? They have even bigger sizes too.

7. **Pink Chicken** showroom on 1223 Madison Ave is paradise shop for little girls that feel like princesses. Invented by Stacy Fraser and her knowledge of fashion (inspired by her daughters), she enabled moms and their girls to pick sweet tutus, dresses, quirky and fashionable pieces and much more. On the plus side, excess clothes are donated to children in need.

8. **My Little Sunshine** is the shop of incredible high-end clothing that is durable foremost. Be amazed by the brands like Tane Organics or Blu Pony Vintage. It is practical, one-stop shop along your daily route – and there is even a children's haircut salon next to it. Can it be more practical than this? Just head to 177 9th Ave.

9. Cristina Villegas from Colombia used her stylist passion to open the gorgeous shop **Yoya** on 605 Hudson St. She sells high-quality, durable and international brands of clothing such as Leoca Paris and Emile et Idea. But, Cristina does not stop here, she also works as an interior kids' room designer as well!

10. Stocked up cute kids' clothes (and items) are displayed in the cutest way possible in **Area Kids.** The clothes are mostly designed by local designers such as Egg & Avocado or Appaman, but you can find some quite interesting pieces with German and French origins. Located at 331 Smith St. Brooklyn. It is a kids' paradise of colors!

Chapter 5

10 Baby Clothes Wholesale Suppliers In The USA

Some of the most popular apparel items today are baby clothes. They are available from wholesale suppliers. These are companies that buy large amounts of baby clothes.

After that, they warehouse them and then sell them to retailers. There are some baby clothes wholesalers who only carry one brand. They are known as distributors. Here are 10 baby clothes wholesale suppliers in the USA.

KIDSBLANKS by ZOE

Located in Santa Ana, California, this is a wholesale company that provides baby clothes to customers in the USA. They have items such as onesies, bibs, dresses, gowns for newborns, girls tops, burp cloths and baby blankets too. KIDSBLANKS also offers customized items through screen printing. They offer brand new and second hand items too.

Penguin Kids Wear Inc.

Based in Los Angeles, California, USA, this company is a leading wholesaler of baby clothes. They have a wide variety of clothing for baby girls and boys. Penguin Kids Wear Inc. is licensed to carry a variety of brands and lines of baby clothing for all ages.

Doodle Pants

This is a baby clothes wholesale company which provides leggings and children's clothing. Located in Cotuit, Massachusetts, USA, this company distributes their products to Independent Retail Stores across the country. They offer individual retail stores the chance to join their network by registering on their website.

Bambini Infant Wear

This wholesaler specializes in providing baby clothing items made of 100% cotton such as infant layette clothing items. Also, they provide baby accessories too. They include basics and specialty items as well. Newborns and infants are provided for in the inventory by Bambini Infant wear. Located in Irvine, California, USA, the company uses the latest textile technologies and top quality materials in making their products.

Infant Blanks

For many years, this company has provided knitted baby clothes to their distributors. They also provide blanks for promotion and embroidery too. Clients can order customized pieces. Moreover, Infant Blanks also services Private Label orders.

Kid's Dream

This is a baby clothes wholesaler that is located in the Los Angeles, California, USA. The company specializes in providing baby clothes for special occasions. Some examples of items that they can provideinclude outfits for christenings, infant dresses, formal attire for boys, accessories and communion outfits as well. Their items are highly fashionable too.

DollarDays

Focusing on providing baby clothes, this is an American company that provides items to special clients. Examples of these are nonprofits and small businesses as well. They also offer these items to individual clients.

Rock Bottom Deals

This wholesaler provides baby clothes at the most affordable prices. They are located in Chicago, Illinois, USA. Some examples of the items that they provide include baby clothes, baby supplies and accessories too. Rock Bottom Deals provides the top brands to their customers.

All USA Clothing

Established in 1970, this is a company that focuses on providing baby clothing which is made and manufactured in the USA. Based in Keego Harbor, Michigan, USA, they provide clothes, shoes and accessories for any size that you desire. They are also capable of providing these items as blank or decorated. In addition to that, All USA Clothing provides original custom designed apparel.

Wholesale Blank Clothes

This is a company that specializes in providing blank clothing at wholesale prices. Based in Austintown, Ohio, the company provides these items at highly affordable prices. They have a variety of baby clothes for their customers.

Chapter 6

10 Wholesale USA And UK Suppliers For Little Girls Clothing

1. Trade Kids Wear

As the name suggests, Trade kids wear is an on line, wholesale supplier of kids clothes, who have an elaborate department that specializes in trendy young girls clothing. According to their website their little girls' clothing are made to compete with recent market trends, and that they are always ahead of the trends by continuously updating their design department. Trade kids wear has split the little girls' section into two; girls younger than 10 years and girls older girls up to 13 years. In stock they have T shirts, leggings, tops, onesies, shorts, jumpers, cardigans, jackets, coats and accessories . Their brands include Minx, soft touch, Hay Wire, Girl Clothing, Disney, Ex- chain store, Bee BO, Baby C, Freaky among others.

2. Kids Blanks

This is an on-line Wholesale sup[plier of little girls' clothing based in Santa Ana, California, USA. Kids Blanks has in stock baby clothing, toddler and youth T-shirts, Onesies, bibs, newborn gowns, dresses, burp cloths, girls tops, beanies hats, Sleep N Play, and diaper covers,. They also do custom manufacturing and screen printing.

3. Dollipops Kidz

Dolli pops kid z is a little girls wholesale boutique that deals in trendy little girls' clothing, They stock pettiskirts, petti rompers, swing top sets, shoes, minky blankets, headbands, bows, dance wear, tuts and dresses. They also offer opportunities for online sellers.

4. Lady Charm Wholesale

This is a US based women's, online wholesale clothing store with a kids department that specializes on little girls clothing. They stock hair bows, baby blankets, T-shirts, 2 piece outfits and dresses.

5. Doodle pants

Doodle Pants is a wholesaler located in Cotuit, Massachusetts in the US. They supply unique kids' leggings and kids clothing to independent retail stores.

6. Kid's dream-Made in USA

Located in downtown Los Angeles, California, USA. Kid"s dream manufactures and wholesales trendy designs in form of special occasion dresses, young girls dresses, infant dresses , christening outfit and accessories. They ship worldwide.

7.Hair Bow Company

The Hairbow company is located in Texas, United States, and specializes in trendy boutique clothing and apparel and quality hair bows for infants and young girls. They also offer free domestic shipping for orders above $150.

8. Adam Sinclair Ltd.

The UK based online store is an international distributor and wholesaler of little girls and boys branded sportswear from Adam Sinclair, Adidas, Nike, Puma, Reebok and other international brands.

9. Angel Wholesale

This is an Award winning Wholesaler from The UK. Angel wholesale specializes in high quality baby clothing, children's clothing and baby products from reputable brands. They stock character line, preschool toys, soft toys, children's clothes, baby shower and baby basket supplies and blanks baby products for customizations. They claim to have over 4500 stocked lines and fast next day dispatch from a 10,oo0 sq ft warehouse.

10. Childrenswearwholesalers.com

This UK store was founded in 1964. Children's wear wholesalers stocks a wide range of children's clothing of course including little girls clothing such as tops, jackets, dresses, jeans, shirts. hoodies, skirts, leggings, trousers, jumpsuits, shorts, t-shirts, pajamas, bathrobes, shoes, necklaces, hats, scares, swimwear and school wear. They also have their own exclusive range of products from licensed famous brands and stores including Ben 10, Spider man, Minnie Mouse, Hello Kitty, Toy Story, Manchester United, Lier Pool among others. They offer occasional discounts.

Chapter 7

How To Buy Closeout Kids Merchandise From Retailers In New York

You can actually buy wholesale and closeout kids clothing directly from retailers.

As you can imagine, retailers want to move their unsold merchandise as quickly as they can, since the longer the unsold inventory stays in their stores, the harder it will be to sell.

So what many stores do, including those that sell children wear, is periodically run super clearance sales on their brand name inventory.

I personally have seen kids clothing by designer brands such as Ralph Lauren, Tommy Hilfiger, Disney, and Nike, at sale prices that brought down the cost per piece below to what the original wholesale price would have been.

You can actually buy some of that merchandise and then resell it on eBay, at your local flea market, through the Amazon FBA program, or in your own shop.

If retailers run sales that allow you to buy their products for 70-90% off the original price you will potentially be buying those items at substantially below the regular wholesale price.

Another method to obtain products from retailers for resale purposes is to approach the store manager or owner and make an offer for any hard to sell items.

Yes, you definitely want to be careful in buying items that someone else is having a hard time selling. Perhaps customers simply no longer want those items.

But on the other hand it's possible that the shop was trying to sell the clothing or toys at too high of a price, or the shop simply didn't have the right clientele for that merchandise, and you can find those customers.

The reason why retail arbitrage does work is because shoppers might not know about the toys being sold in one store, and that the store might not know how to market the toys to those customers.

That is actually the reason why so many Amazon sellers engage in arbitrage.

Online sellers know that Amazon is frequented by people from all over the world, giving them a better chance to sell kids merchandise that a local business was having a hard time to move.

Below are 25 retailers that focus on kids products.

I would recommend that you approach each business on the list and inquire as to what products you can buy from them at closeout prices.

As you might know, New Yorkers are no doubt one of the most fashionable city dwellers in the world; and not just adults, you can see toddlers and young boys and girls flaunting the latest trends in their own individual styles.

Parents are always concerned about their children's appearance, especially if they look acceptable when they step out of the house. If you are looking for kids clothing stores to give your young children trendy, fashionable lifestyles, whether it's casual wear, party clothes or shoes, you need to look no further. Here we give you a list of the top 25 New York shops for fashionable clothing for all ages of children; toddlers, kindergarteners, school kids and all other ages!

Since these retailers are doing business in a very competitive market, they are expected to have high quality products.

For Babies and Toddlers

Area Kids

This shop stocks local designers such as Egg & Avocado and Appaman, but another attraction for kids are the creative toys imported from France and Germany. It is located conveniently at 99th Seventh Avenue in Brooklyn. For more details go to https://area-kids.myshopify.com/

Giggle

This dream everything-in-one stop located at 352 Amsterdam Avenue New York for babies and toddlers has a stroller parking area, changing tables inside the store, product demonstrations and organic cotton toys. All the clothing, furniture and equipment is designed keeping in mind new parent's concerns such as space saving ability, ease of washing and durability. Browse through the adorable babies stuff online at http://www.giggle.com/

Pottery Barn Kids

This store stocks home-furnishings exclusively for tykes with so many options for nursery furniture and fittings as well as blankets, playroom accessories and toys. The store is located at 1311 Second Avenue and is a must visit. Check out all the baby products online at http://www.potterybarnkids.com/

Pink Olive

The store is filled with a range of products from Barneys giving parents of babies and toddlers a range of chic clothes and accessories. Some cute accessories include Liberty of London hair bows available for only $16; bear-claw booties for $52 and onesies for $32.

Mini Jake

You can get ultra-modern designs of latest bags, strollers and cribs at 178 North 9th Street in Brooklyn. Available brands include Ouef, Argington and Bloom. Parents can also find helpful stuff for playtime and gifts for friends' babies and toddlers. Shop online at http://www.minijake.com/

Torly Kid

Located at 51 Hudson Street in New York, this store is a one stop shop for tots and tweens which stocks best-selling lines which include Toody Doo, Lunchbos and Appaman for small and big kids. A nice addition is an extensive collection of party favors. Check out their collections at https://torlykid.com/

Kisan

Housing brands like Bonpoint Bonbon and Simple Kids, parents can choose from an array of racks for their babies and toddlers. This store is located at 125 Greene Street in New York. Visit their website for options https://www.kisanstore.com/

Babesta Threads

This cozy 450 square foot store has Junk food t-shirts, Uglydolls, easy bean chairs and vintage wear for all the special kids who want clothes from here. You can specifically buy play mats and teethers and pull-along toys for your babies and toddlers.

This special store is located at 66 West Broadway between Murray and Warren Streets. While more popularly known for children under 6 years of age, it has recently began to stock brands such as Cattauis and Chaos Recycled which cater to older kids. The beautiful stocks here will sure make all adults envious! Visit http://babesta.com/ for details.

Buy Buy Baby

You can choose from a huge variety of pacifiers, bibs and washcloths as well as diaper bags and bedding. Other necessary items for parents with babies and toddlers available here include strollers (ranging from affordable to more expensive models) and complete nursery set-ups with cribs and bed sheets. Go to 270 Seventh Avenue or visit the website https://www.buybuybaby.com/

Sweet William

The owner, a children's fashion editor turned entrepreneur Bronagh Staley is an enthusiast who picks all the stocks herself. She stocks kids clothing, accessories and toys for newborns to kids who are 8 years old. Her favorite brands include April Showers and Wovenplay. Her store is located at 324 Wythe Avenue and is designed with reclaimed wood work that is both sophisticated for adults and attractive for kids. To browse through all her available products go to https://sweetwilliamltd.com/

Lulu's Then and Now

This store at 187, 4th Avenue, Park Slope in Brooklyn is an eco-friendly place which offers slightly used clothing, second hand baby accessories, toys and books. You can bring your little ones to explore the Play Space that is equipped with a library and toys which is open from 10 am to 10 pm and from 2 pm to 5 pm every day and costs only $12 for each session. To see their products go to http://lulusthenandnow.nyc/

Z'Baby Company

This shop was created to cater to a child's personal lifestyle by its founder, Sharone Glaser who stocks clothes for all children starting from infants to preteens exclusively from her own fashion line. The store is located at 100 W 72nd Street in New York and is quite popular amongst those with both boys and girls. Visit the website for details https://zbabycompany.com/

Tiny You

This boutique, located in Long Island stocks local designers with colorful prints that will make your toddlers the life of the party! This shop is located at 10-50 Jackson Avenue in

Queens. Go to their website for more details: http://www.shoptiny.nyc/

Babies R' Us

This chain of baby stores stocks everything you could ever need for your baby: you can choose from the humongous collections of products to feed, bathe, clothe and entertain your little bundle of joy. Products range from the basic and affordable brands to the more luxurious and expensive products from Bugaboo and Timi & Leslie. The store at 24-30 Union Square East has just about everything you and your baby need. Alternatively visit the website for online browsing and shopping at http://www.toysrus.com/shop/index.jsp?categoryId=2255957

Little O Clothing

Little O Clothing lines are 100% hand-sewn in the garment district of New York. The brand focuses on detail oriented heirloom pieces which are high quality and exclusive to this shop only. The clothes are designed to last through periods of toddlers and children's growth so you don't have to regularly replace these outfits.

Little O Clothing is exclusive, well made, easy-to-wear and offered at approachable prices. In an effort to produce ethically and sustainably, the fabric is comprised of organic material and the dyes are derived from natural pigments. Shop online at http://www.littleonyc.com/

Clothing for your Little Princess

Pink Chicken

The creator Stacy Fraser houses a dreamland of beautiful dresses for young girls located at 1223 Madison Avenue in New York. There are so many options for girls ranging from cute casual wear to flouncy party wear are incredibly hard to resist. To check out the beautiful stock go to https://www.pinkchicken.com/

Les Petits Chapelais

Pint sized clothing at this store is so adorable! The stock ranges from shoes, pants and shirts that capture the French spirit. The store is at 86 Thompson Street in New York. Check out the clothes on Facebook at https://www.facebook.com/Les-Petits-Chapelais-NYC-198481876863560/

Infinity

Infinity has been a popular store for girls' clothing for adolescent teens and young ladies. The store at 1116 Madison Avenue is as fashionable as the clothes it stocks! It houses its own brand called Hollyworld and probably has the best customer service amongst all the stores on the Upper East Side. If they don't have what you want, you can even order custom made clothing for yourself! Visit the store if you want to get yourself, your daughter or friend high end fashionable outfits at reasonable prices or visit the website http://infinityonmadisonny.com/

Little Miss Matched

A great store for young girls and tweens is Little Miss Matched at 107 E 42nd Street, Grand Central Station on Lexington Passage. As you enter you are greeted with the bright and colorful array of girly accessories, socks, stockings, dresses and other clothing. Customer reviews rate the service as friendly and helpful. Visit their website at http://littlemissmatched.com/

All Dressed Up

This store is located at 17 Rye Ridge Plaza, Westchester, NY and is a haven for girl's party dresses. You can also find dresses for formal and special occasions such as proms and weddings at this store. See the website at http://shopalldressedup.com/

Shop for the Little Boys

Denny's Childrenswear

With many locations in New York, this store provides clothing for boys of all ages. If you want to get formal attire for special occasions for your son, nephew or other boys this is the place for you. Denny's also has an online store at http://dennyschildrenswear.com

Sir Lance's Lot

Located at 6277 Woodhaven Boulevard in Rego Park, NY, this store offers special outfits for boys ranging three piece suits and even costumes for parties. Go to the website http://sirlanceslot.net/

Jacardi Paris

This is a popular brand for chic, smart and sophisticated clothing for all kids. Customer reviews specifically point to satisfaction with the store's high quality boys' clothing. It has several stores all over New York and also stocks its clothing at Barney's. Visit the website to peruse through the collections for boys at https://www.jacadi.us/

Top Unisex stores for children's clothing in New York

TaROO Too

This chic children's boutique is located at 1480 First Avenue; one street away from the original TaROO on the Upper Street Side and stocks clothing for girls and boys from ages 14 to 16 years. You can mix and match trendy brands such as Mudpie, Lemon and Charlie Rocket which start at just $8.

Free events are also regularly organized which invite customers to participate in glitter-tattoo parties and karaoke events during the week.

For more details visit their website: http://www.taroonyc.com/

Two Kids and a Dog

There are so many varieties of kids clothing, toys, shoes and accessories as well as birthday gifts for presents. It is located at 61 Pearl St in New York. The Brooklyn based owners, Natalia and Kip also provide a lot of repping gear for toddlers such as onesies and t-shirts for toddlers. They stock popular brands such as Joah Love and Chaser that are so loved by kids!

For more options and information go to https://twokidsandadog.com/collections

Bit'z Kids

If you want Japanese clothing, shoes and toys this is definitely the place to go! Your kids can romp around in the play area equipped with both diaper-changing and breastfeeding room. The main store is located at 410 Columbus Avenue. It stocks brands such as the NYC collection and Indigo. Check out their website for more information: https://www.bitzkidsnyc.com/

Crewcuts

This line is from J.Crew especially developed for kids who can opt for the collegiate look of blazers, cardigans and chinos for boys as well as different types of skirts for girls. Their flagship store is located at 1190 Madison Avenue, New York. Go on their website https://www.jcrew.com for browsing through their collection.

My Little Sunshine

This one stop shop at 177 Ninth Avenue in New York stocks high end brands such as Blu Pony Vintage and Tane Organics as well as a selection of toys, books and a creative haircut station for kids. Check out their stock on http://www.mylittlesunshinenyc.com/

Yoya

This high end store sells international brands like Emile et Idea and Leoca Paris. It also stocks children's furniture and bedding and provides design consulting for kid's rooms

It is located at 605 Hudson Street in New York. Visit their website: http://www.yoyanyc.com/

Little Marc Jacobs

This is truly a miniature version of the Marc Jacobs brand; ready to wear collections for boys and girls feature skirts and cool leather jackets. Go to the store at 298 W 4th Street in New York for your little ones or visit the website: https://www.marcjacobs.com/kids/

Egg by Susan Lazar

If you are environmentally conscious and prefer organic materials for yourself and your kids, go to 72 Jay Street in Brooklyn for simple colors, fabrics and prints. Or visit their website to see the collections: http://www.egg-baby.com/

Junior Lowe

The online tagline says that the collection is for little Brooklyn hipsters' which offers plaid shirts for small boys. Situated at 89 Atlantic Avenue in Brooklyn you can browse through several options for your fashion conscious boys. See more at http://jrlowe.com/

Level 2

Looking for hip styles for your young ones? Go to 456 Bergen Street in Brooklyn. This is the place to shop! You can find patterned dresses from Miss Behave, bright t-shirts designed by Stella Blu and denim clothes by Tractr. Also see the funky accessories like wallets and sunglasses for your kids.

Bonpoint

Looking for French très chic clothing for your children? Go to Bonpoint for apparel shopping for toddlers and tweens at its many outlets; the main store is located at 1269 Madison Avenue and another one in Soho. Go online at http://www.bonpoint.com/us/ for more details.

Magic Windows

For over 32 years, this Upper East Side store located at 1186 Madison Avenue has been dressing New York kids for parties and special occasions. Their stocks include different colored frocks for girls and smart collars for boys. Check out their website http://magicwindowskids.com/

Lucy & Leo

With organic material, the soft and stretchable clothing for kids has made this environmentally and health conscious brand very popular amongst both parents and kids! The garments are all locally manufactured and the store also offers mother and baby skincare products as well as toys and accessories all made from organic sources. Lucy and Leo stocks in the New York store of Wild was Mama which is located at 272 Driggs Avenue in Brooklyn. For more detail of their clothing and other products, go to https://www.wildwasmama.com/

Half Pint Citizens

The store location is as hip as it sounds: it is situated at 55 Washington Street in DUMBO, Brooklyn. This store stocks an amazing specialty of unique and fashionable clothes. Customers rate the dresses for girls as especially beautiful. Check out the hippest clothes for kids on their website at http://www.halfpintcitizens.com/

Boutique for Children

For the style conscious parents and children, this store at 71-21 Austin Street in Forest Hills, NY is the place to go for shopping! It stocks a wide variety of high quality trendy clothing with excellent customer service. The brands include designers such as Armani, Diesel and Burberry. You can definitely choose your kids outfits for special occasions from this stylish store. Visit http://www.boutiqueforchildren.com/

Lester's

Lester's has five locations in New York (Manhattan, Brooklyn, Westchester and Long Island) and is the ultimate go-to shop for children's fashion. It houses designer brands and latest fashions for kids. See their clothing at http://lestersnyc.com/

Neils Corner Spot

This store, located at 1063 Wills Avenue, Albertson, NY has every kids' outfits for every occasion and season. You can even buy swimwear, camp wear and casual clothing here. Check out the website at http://neilscornerspot.com/

Smoochie Baby

This store located at 110 Berry Street between North 7th and North 8th Streets houses brands such as Appaman, Egg, Cupcakes and Pastries, Native Kids and Salt Water foot wear. In addition to clothes, it also stocks accessories for toddlers. Visit https://smoochiebaby.com/ for more info.

Kidding Around

Located at 60 West 15th Street near Sixth Avenue NY, this shop is a heaven for toys and funky costumes for kids The toy collection is especially attractive for kids. Visit the website at http://www.kiddingaroundnyc.com/

L.O.L. Kids

This boutique, located at 22 West 21st Street between Fifth and Sixth Avenues carries European brands for kids up to 16 years of age, especially in pink and lace for girls. Go to http://www.lol-kids.com/

Get Fashionable Shoes for your Kids!

Naturino

This shoe store caters to fitting the growing feet of kids through its line Falcotto which is especially made for toddlers who are learning to walk and for older kids inspired by latest footwear trends for adults. The store is located at 1184 Madison Avenue and the collections can be viewed online at https://www.naturino.com/en_en/

Space Kiddets

This store offers funky shoes, shirts and toys for toddlers as well as bigger kids. It is located at 26 E 22nd Street in New York. Visit the website for more information: http://www.spacekiddets.com/

Tip Top Shoes

This adult shoe store has a kids-only location at 155 W 72nd Street NY and has an extensive collection for little ones ranging from sandals to moccasins. Check out their stocks at http://tiptopshoes.com/

Soula Shoes

This shoe store located at 85 North 3rd Street in Brooklyn stocks a versatile collection of cool converse, Timberlands and Hunters for play time. See the website at https://soulashoes.com/

Ibiza Kidz

You can find standard kids foot wear at this store at 830 Broadway in New York like Crocs and Keds and shop for dressier and formal footwear including ballet flats and dainty sandals. See their products at http://ibizakidz.com/

Kids Foot Locker

You can get running shoes, sneakers and may more options from brands ranging from Nike, Adidas, Puma and New Balance. You can visit the store at 5314 Fifth Avenue in Brooklyn or shop online at http://www.kidsfootlocker.com

6. Village Kids Footwear

You can choose comfortable shoes for your kids that range from brands such as Clark and Pediped for toddlers and kids up to shoe size 7. Go to the store at 117 First Avenue in New York or visit the website at http://kidsshoesmanhattanny.wixsite.com/villagekids

7. Harry's Shoes for Kids

Located at 2315 Broadway, NY this store provides individual customer service helping parents to measure and evaluate the fit of shoes for kids. It stocks popular brands such as Merrell, Stride Rite and Ugg and offers shoes for all types of weather and purposes. Browse through the collections online at http://www.harrys-shoes.com/default.aspx

8. Stride Rite

Renowned for the fit and durability of kids' shoes, this chain is a one-stop shop for socks, tights and other accessories. It stocks brands like Sperry and Saucony as well as specific shoes for school. Themed shoes from popular kids' television shows and animated movies such as Sesame Street, Frozen and Disney Princesses are also available. To check out their products online go to https://www.timeout.com/new-york-kids/shopping/stride-rite

9. Runnin' Wild Kids Shoes

This Brooklyn shop offers the newest styles and brands of shoes imaginable! The stocks include brands such as Skechers, Geox, Superga and Puma. The staff is extremely professional and friendly and will help you choose the right shoe style and fit for your child. The store is located at 276 Court Street in Brooklyn. You can visit the website at http://runninwildkidshoes.tumblr.com/

10. DSW

This store, with many locations across New York, has a huge variety of kids and adult shoes. DSW has shoes for every occasion: formal shoes for kids, sneakers, sandals and so many other styles, ranging between $25 and $60. You can visit the DSW designer shoe warehouse at 79th and Broadway or shop online at http://stores.dsw.com/usa/ny/brooklyn/dsw-designer-shoe-warehouse-atlantic-terminal.html

11. Macy's Herald Square

This store has a huge section of shoes for kids for everyday wear and special occasions. Visit the store with the most amazing selection at 151 W 34th Street NY or visit the website at http://macys.com/

12. Popular Retail Outlets for Children of All Ages:

You can also opt for the well-known brands such as Nordstrom, Bloomingdale's, and H&M which stock clothes for all ages of kids.

13. Nordstrom

This popular store houses hundreds of brands for kids ranging from the high end like Burberry to other more affordable labels. You can easily browse through the collections online in the comfort of your home at http://shop.nordstrom.com/c/kids-brands/all

14. H&M

This brand is popular for both its affordability and practicality. It stocks clothes for practically all ages, from newborns to 14 year olds and of course adults. Dresses for girls can be as low as $4.99 during special deals and sale periods which is a godsend for anyone with children. There are many stores in New York that you can visit or see http://www.hm.com/us/department/KIDS

15. Macy's

This is a one-stop shop for adults and kids featuring every product of clothing conceivable: shoes, toys, dresses, t-shirts, you name it and you can find it at Macy's. Again, there are several retail stores and the option of shopping online at https://www.macys.com/shop/kids-clothes?id=5991

16. Bloomingdale's

This retail store operating throughout the US and New York offers a wide variety of clothing for kids. Collections are sold for each season, style and occasion which makes it much easier for parents. Visit a retail outlet or shop online at https://www.bloomingdales.com/shop/kids?id=3866

17. Target

This chain also offers pretty delicate dresses for girls and rough and tumble t-shirts and shorts for boys at affordable prices. You can visit the store or go check out the girls collection online at http://intl.target.com/c/girls-clothing/-/N-5xtwa

18. Gymboree

With multiple stores all over New York and the country, this high end kids clothing brand offers apparel and accessories for children at its original outlets and stocks in other stores such as Janie and Jack and Crazy 8. Customers are happy with the high quality and unique clothing, especially for kids aged 12 and under. And you can take advantage of the sales and amazing deals for members. They also arrange special activities for parents and children like painting and dancing. Go to http://www.gymboree.com/

19. Barneys New York

Another popular retailer is Barney's New York which has a seemingly unlimited stock of kids clothing, accessories and toys and gifts for all children. Their most popular store in New York is located at 660 Madison Avenue on the Upper East Side. Visit the store or go to their website to browse through at http://www.barneys.com/category/kids/N-cwqgiq

20. Brooklyn Industries

This adult clothing chain also stocks a fashionable collection of kids wear. You can shop for hip and trendy t-shirts, sweatshirts and onesies at the North Williamsburg store or the Southberg Outlet. Check out the website at http://www.brooklynindustries.com/

Secondhand Clothing Stores for Kids in New York

Parents are always in search of good bargains for their growing kids and most do not want to dole too much money for clothing that their child will outgrow in the next season. Going to consignment stores and thrift shops is a good alternative to expensive kids clothing. The fun part about going to these stores is that you will find such gems that are not available in big chain stores and your child will stand out from the crowd. Often these stores also stock children's gear, such as toys, books and bed rails that you can pass from your eldest child to the youngest one.

Here are a few viable secondhand store options that you can visit in New York City:

Clementine

Located in Greenwich Village at 39 Washington Square South, this is a consignment store that stocks literally every kind of clothing for kids and expectant mothers. Two local mothers, Cara Walla and Myrle opened this shop because there was no consignment clothing available in the area.

You can browse through the wide variety of stock that is available for extremely reasonable prices. In addition, you can also drop your kids used clothing and earn 40% of the sale price.

Flying Squirrel

This spacious boutique located at 87 Oak Street in Greenpoint provides a huge selection of kids clothing, toys and furniture for babies as well as expecting mothers. There is also a playroom for kids while their parents browse the collections. Events are also organized for special occasions such as Halloween. You can donate used clothes here too.

Once Upon a Child

Located in Staten Island on 2305 Richmond Avenue near Shiloh Street this store is one of a country wide chain of second hand outlets which sells and buys children's clothing, toys, furniture and shoes. You can bring in gently used items and be paid 30 to 50% of the resale price on the spot.

Jane's Exchange

Designed specifically for those on a tight budget or don't want to spend too much on kids clothes, Jane's Exchange at 191 E 3rd Street New York is a must visit. The used clothes are in good condition for both kids and expecting mothers. See http://www.janesexchangenyc.com/

With the wide variety of retail and shops in NYC, you will have no difficulty in shopping for cool and hip closeout and liquidation deals. Just remember, that although these businesses are not wholesale suppliers, they are eager to sell out their shelf pulls and remainders. It is up to you to contact them and make them a below wholesale offer for their inventory.

Conclusion

I hope you enjoyed this guide on how to buy wholesale and closeout kids' merchandise in New York.

You are welcome to visit my wholesale warehouse the next time you are in New York!

My website is www.closeoutexplosion.com

You can reach me directly at my cell phone/WhatsApp number 1-917-913-6093

I would be happy to try to answer any questions that you might have.

www.ingramcontent.com/pod-product-compliance
Lightning Source LLC
Chambersburg PA
CBHW030736180526
45157CB00008BA/3201